Delores Johnson

EDGAR D. LAWRENCE

MINISTERING TO THE SILENT MINORITY

Gospel Publishing House
Springfield, Missouri
02-0738

Library of Congress Catalog Card Number 78-55679
International Standard Book Number 0-88243-738-0

Printed in the United States of America

ACKNOWLEDGMENTS

Appreciation is expressed to the following who have provided relevant input and feedback directly from the active ministerial field.

Rev. James Banks, national representative for the Deaf and Blind Ministries, Division of Home Missions of the Assemblies of God, and Rev. T. E. Gannon, national Home Missions Director of the same organization, provided the initial impetus for the production of this book.

Ministers to the deaf who read the manuscript and made suggestions are Rev. and Mrs. Lloyd Couch, Rev. and Mrs. Fred Gravatt, Joanne Lambert, Dorothy Scott, Jeanne Manning, and Jacob Trout, Jr. Others who read the manuscript expressed appreciation for such a needed text.

Wayne Warner and David J. Johnston gave encouragement and assisted in the production.

DEDICATED TO

My colleagues and fellow ministers whose steadfast determination and commitment to the deaf has led multitudes to Christ, who shall rise up and call them "blessed" in THAT DAY . . . .

Preface

The book you are about to read is one that has evolved from the great need of several years for some basic information to underscore the already existent ongoing ministry to the deaf. Year after year I have been deluged with both written and verbal requests for "how-to-do-it" information as well as basic information relating to the deaf and ministry to them.

Although I am an ordained minister in the Assemblies of God, I have attempted to keep a nondenominational viewpoint in the hopes of making it profitable to any and all who are challenged to this great harvest field.

The material presented is written in an understandable style with a concerted effort to deprofessionalize the jargon and technical language found in many publications.

The intent of this book is to help students, teachers, ministers, and other professionals who may contemplate ministry to the deaf to better understand their target population.

E. Lawrence

Contents

1
Ministry to the Deaf

A basic question a missionary asks prior to entering a specific geographical area of ministry is, "Are there people there?" The average American minister, unless he has had contact with deaf persons in some way, is unaware there is a *population* he cannot reach without special assistance from trained personnel not already on his staff. More will be said later about ways of meeting this need in the local church. Suffice it to say at this point that the National Census of the Deaf of 1970 (completed in 1973) shocked even those whose estimates of the deaf population were supposedly generous.

The average minister, when approached regarding a ministry to the deaf in his church, wants to know what potential size congregation he can expect. There are 13.4 million persons in the U.S. who have an impairment of hearing. Of these, 1.8 million are deaf and about 0.4 million became deaf before 19 years of age.[1]

These figures are confusing to the average pastor, so translated into common terms, there are two deaf and/or hearing-impaired per 1000 population of your community. In addition, large metropolitan areas may have an even higher concentration of deaf due to employment opportunities in industries and businesses. So, if you are a minister in such an area your potential congregation could be well above the two-per-thousand rate.

American Annuals identified 503 churches or synagogues of all denominations for the deaf in the U.S. and 15 in Canada. This means there are 25,888 deaf or hearing-impaired for each church; however, the sad truth is that it is a rare church for the deaf that averages 100 or over in attendance.

Such statistics are overwhelming when we see the great multitude who are not being ministered to.

It has always intrigued me that missionaries are excited and challenged to go to a foreign field for labor, constrained by the opportunity of presenting the gospel to a tribe or people who have "never heard," yet we have the deaf neglected religiously "everywhere" in the United States. Many have had only a superficial exposure to Christianity, consisting mainly of Sunday school classes in the residential deaf school taught by some who did not even profess a religious preference, to say nothing of a "religious experience."

Since 1965 the public has become increasingly aware of the neglected, prejudiced, and discriminative situation of the deaf in the U.S. Although great strides have been made to improve the educational and vocational level of the deaf, we have not seen this in the religious world. It would be interesting (although probably impossible to document) to trace the religious educational opportunities of the deaf during the past 200 years in the U.S. Since education of the deaf dates back to only about 1850, it is obvious no religious instruction occurred to any degree prior to that time.

The following excerpt from a speech by Dr. David M. Denton deals with this problem.*

Total Communication—The Spiritual Dimension

If we are able to fully embrace the philosophy of Total Communication, then we must recognize that all dimensions of the deaf child's existence must be considered—including the spiritual dimension. I am deeply concerned about what I consider to be one of the most neglected areas in the lives of so many of our deaf citizens, including both children and adults. Sometimes it seems that we, as professional people, become so engrossed in the other dimensions of a deaf person's existence that religious or spiritual development is given extremely low priority or is completely forgotten. More, not less, effort is required in meeting the spiritual needs of deaf children and adults than is true of hearing people. This relates, of course, to the problem of communication. Those basic, but not so important spiritual, moral, and religious concepts and principles must be introduced early into the life of a deaf child, and this, of course, must be done in a way that is understandable and useful by the child himself. Relevance and personal involvement in the spiritual area is as important as it is in the academic area. Basic to this, of course, is the obvious fact that the family must be able to provide a personal, spiritual involvement for the deaf member of the family. Perhaps this should be a part of parent counseling while the child is still young.

Before going further, let me identify for you what I consider to be three major problem areas in existing religious services and programs for deaf people. These problem areas involve what we could term Quantity, Quality, and Style. The first and most obvious deals with the number of religious programs available for deaf people. The problem is that too few churches on a national and local level provide a program for religious involvement for deaf persons. The

*From a speech given at the annual Dan Cloud Memorial Award Program at California State University, Northridge, August 2, 1972. Dr. Denton is superintendent of the Maryland State School for the Deaf. Used by permission.

need, of course, is for a new level of sensitivity and responsiveness on the part of organized religious groups to fully embrace and totally involve deaf people as active and responsive members of the church congregation. The second deals with the quality of many existing religious services for the deaf. Too many of them still continue to institutionalize deaf worshipers by separating them into a special group, or by providing opportunities for participation in only part of the total worship experience. Far too frequently the membership of a local church is aware only of the physical interaction. It is almost as if the deaf persons were considered non-persons. Perhaps we need to be jolted into a realization that deaf people, not only have something to get from the worship, but they also have much to give.

Number three deals with the style or pattern of typical church programs for the deaf. They tend to follow the pattern of passive or spectator type of participation rather than personal involvement. Someone interpreting a sermon is much better than nothing, but is it adequate to bring the deaf members into full spiritual fellowship? Another characteristic of traditional programs is that they tend to group deaf persons of all ages together and treat them as a single group, with a single need. Churches must begin to minister to deaf persons of all ages from nursery school onward. Whatever a church provides the regular membership should also be made available to the deaf. To consider the concept of education or rehabilitation without considering man's spiritual dimension, is to deny one of the fundamental truths of human existence. Perhaps it seems strange that I, as an educator, am standing before you talking about spiritual development of deaf people. Perhaps it is strange, but I feel very strongly that if we do not first look to **ourselves** for leadership, then to whom do we look? If asked what my biggest concern for the future was, I would have to answer that it involves the growing insensitivity to the need for nurturing our children's spiritual lives and the seeming unwillingness of our social institutions to provide children with a set of moral, spiritual values sufficient to sustain them during times of personal crisis and sufficient to prepare them for lives of responsible service to the other people. I am not talking about the doctrinal nor theological aspects of religion, but rather of the recognition that deaf people do have souls.

When a pastor considers adding a ministry to the deaf to his church's responsibilities he must consider his motivation seriously and objectively. His desire to do so must go far beyond the beauty and sometimes "novelty" of the language of signs. A greater number added to the church membership roster is probably the poorest motivating factor. Many aspects must be considered which will be dealt with in more detail in subsequent chapters.

To name a few (lest this be the only chapter the pastor reads) consider these questions:

1. Do I (or we) truly desire to minister to and have a burden of responsibility for the deaf?
2. Is this church ready to support a ministry to the deaf financially, facility-wise, and spiritually?
3. Do we have adequate facilities for worship, education, and caring for the children of deaf parents?
4. Are we prepared to provide specially trained interpreters and/or ministers to the deaf on their educational, language, and vocabulary level?
5. Are we willing to provide additional visual aids and equipment as needed to overcome the communication barrier in presenting the gospel to the deaf?

If the church is not ready to subscribe to these issues at least in a nominal, cooperative way and look to God "for the increase," then it would probably be better to leave the ministry to the deaf to a neighboring pastor with a burden for it.

The preceding statement may seem rather harsh, but historically the deaf have been exploited and they are very wary of new church groups which may be unstable and dissolve as rapidly as they appeared, leaving the deaf parishioners bewildered, confused, and deeply disappointed. In considering the strongest, ongoing churches for the deaf nationwide, we find they are pastored by men and women who have persevered and stayed through the years, laying the foundation and building thereon. Vacillating, insecure, insincere ministers should not attempt a ministry to the deaf—to do so only brings reproach to the gospel and wreaks havoc in the church.

If you are still sincerely interested in the deaf, I encourage you to read further and give yourself a brief basis of knowledge regarding these fascinating, exciting, lovable, unreached people called *the deaf!*

2

The Call and Training for Deaf Ministry

After having been enlightened about the overwhelming need for deaf ministry, people often ask: "How do I know whether I am called to minister to the deaf?" My first reply is: "The same way you know you are a Christian!" There is a deep conviction within your heart and mind that God wants you to minister to this special segment of humanity.

I must hasten to say that the "call" alone is not sufficient for successful ministry. I have seen some enroll in college—"called to the deaf"—only to find themselves unable to absorb even the very basics of communication and knowledge regarding the deaf. Only God can call a person, but we as fellow laborers can at least evaluate the situation and counsel those persons to perhaps become assistants or helpers to those who have become proficient in this area. Academia alone certainly does not qualify one for ministry, but neither does ignorance! If God really called, He will give the enablement.

Surely one called to deaf ministry must first be *called* to the "ministry" in general. The special call to the deaf may not manifest itself in a "light from heaven," "audible voice," vision in sign language, or other exotic experience. It may be a *developing* call.

Many of those now ministering to the deaf became interested in the ministry by exposure to deaf persons on college campuses or other places. Some learned sign language as an added mode of communication, only to become intrigued by the deaf and learn to love and appreciate them. Then they felt led by God to minister to them.

If one feels "called" to minister to the deaf he or she should examine his motives seriously. Years ago in a workshop situation I met a lady who had formed an organization to help the deaf. It sounded like a charity-welfare group and I shall never forget her or the literature she distributed to help "these poor unfortunate deaf." Her attitude was condescending to say the least, but her tone was one of abject pity for the "poor unfortunate deaf!" Individuals who minister only out of pity are apt to be of little help to those they are trying to aid.

Some people have been reluctant to prepare for deaf ministry because they felt to do so would mean total abandonment of "hearing" friends and total immersion into the subculture of the deaf. This is not true. Many are successfully ministering to both audiences.

Psychologically a hearing person needs to hear sounds, voices, music, etc. To subject oneself to total silence destroys the equilibrium God has given us (called homeostasis by psychologists).

In summation, a call may be, but need not be, a revelatory experience. The call to deaf ministry should not be considered a "lesser ministry," but a more specific ministry to a special group of people; nor should it leave one with a feeling he must change his whole hearing orientation.

I have both heard and read that one should not go into the ministry if he or she could be happy doing anything else. Initially I was in disagreement with that philosophy but the older I become the greater my agreement. I have met several people who are still in the pulpit ministering to the deaf but are very unhappy. I say, "Leave the pulpit so the deaf can be ministered to by those who truly enjoy ministering to them!"

A. G. Ward summed it up well when he said: "The minister after God's own heart is one who holds his credentials from heaven, who knows he is called of God, and who feels that he dare not attempt any other work than preaching the gospel."[2]

Although we must deal separately with these two subjects—the call and the training—in actuality they are inseparable! Some individuals receive a *call* while very young and must wait until they graduate from high school, attend college, etc., before attaining their goal. Others, having received a general call to full-time ministry, prepare by training at a Bible college or seminary and there become involved in this deaf ministry.

It matters not which way you enter, but be assured *training* is necessary. Many deaf groups have been started by zealous, well-intentioned persons who make havoc of the church because of inadequate preparation. Some individuals learn the language of signs for a novelty and thus infer that deaf ministry is just "so much fun," only to discover they cannot personally cope with the frustrations, crises, and frankness of the deaf world.

First, let us look at some considerations that must be taken into account when we think of training for deaf ministry: (1) immediate need; (2) available finances and facilities; (3) long-range goals; and, (4) time available for adequate training.

Training for ministry to the deaf has for far too long consisted of a series of lessons in sign language. We are somehow given the impression that if a person can proficiently sign to the deaf he can immediately minister to them by merely signing what is taught, preached, or spoken to his hearing friends. Nothing is further from the truth! And to use the ability to sign in such a way may bring immediate rebuke as well as confusion to a deaf group. It is but the *first step.*

Training must, of necessity, begin with the language. I know of no one who is an expert on whether short-term or long-term training in signs is best. That decision must rest on my first point above, "immediate need." Years ago while preparing to leave my pastorate, one fine Christian lady wanted to learn signs before I left (in 4 weeks) so she could minister to the deaf after my departure. We spent many 3- and 4-hour afternoon sessions together to meet this *immediate need.* She learned rapidly and still interprets for the deaf in that church. This is an example of successful short-term training.

I am not convinced, however, that short-term sign language training (a 2- or 3-week course) is adequate, but it is surely better than no training at all. And occasional workshops and/or seminars would enrich such a program. In many areas it is the *only* answer to meet the growing need of interpreters, workers, and ministers to the deaf. However, I believe those who do conduct this type of program are responsible to orient the trainees in regard to deafness and the deaf world. Certainly, without the short-term programs conducted by some organizations or churches ministers to the deaf would be in short supply. When a church or person cannot afford to spend thousands of dollars and 4 years in preparation, such short-term programs are needful.

Being involved in a Bible college program has certainly convinced me that long-term training is the *ideal* way to go—although, admittedly, slow and expensive. In conjunction with the normal Bible college curricula, one can add training in ministry to the deaf and gain the further plus of having 4 years of exposure and social interchange with the deaf in the college and/or community. During this 4 years comes maturity which lessens the frustrations of deaf ministry. Such a program can easily project long-term goals, and after 4 years a regular supply (though always insufficient in number) of trained ministers to the deaf will evolve. Then if a local church discovers a need for someone to minister to the deaf, contacting such a training program may yield the needed personnel. Be they religious organizations or otherwise, those who are successful with ongoing programs for the deaf are those with adequate training!

Training programs are only as good as the administration and teachers themselves. I have never been able to understand why those least proficient in signs always envision themselves as "experts." In all kindness to beginning sign language students, I always say, "No one knows more about sign language than the student who has been in class 6 weeks!" May this serve as counsel for those who say, "All the deaf sign it that way!"

The teacher of sign language should be careful to sign clearly and correctly. A teacher who signs carelessly produces students who sign carelessly. I have signed for over 20 years and I still see new signs I have never seen before. So, it is wise never to say, "That is wrong—this is right," but rather, "That may be the sign in your geographical area but the sign I use is this."

If one teacher is conducting the entire class, it is wise to prepare material regarding deafness to be interspersed throughout the lesson. This will help to break the monotony of the class as well as orient them to deafness. If time does not permit, a printed handout of information could be given. Many times questions will naturally develop and that is the opportune time to answer them!

The purpose of this book precludes instruction on how to teach sign language but the obvious trend today is to use Total Communication, i.e. signs, voice, hearing aids, lipreading, gestures, visuals, pantomime—everything possible to *communicate!* Teaching signs in contextual sentences is a valid and proven method and helps retain vocabulary more easily than by word lists.[3]

A few words need to be said regarding the various sign systems in use throughout the country today. S.E.E. (Seeing Essential English or Seeing Exact English) or L.O.V.E. (Linguistics of Visual English) and Signed English all have the basic goal of communication with the deaf with the further goal of teaching them better English language patterns. These basic sign forms are being used primarily in educational settings with the goal of teaching language to deaf children.

Should such children attend your church it would be well to adopt their system for Sunday school classroom instruction with the goal of total understanding. However, the *general adult* population in the deaf world is not familiar with or desirous of changing lifelong sign language patterns because "hearing people" want them to. In teaching signs and preparing others for deaf ministry teach basic sign language and leave the more complex sign systems for educational use.

Clarification needs to be made regarding the language of signs in foreign countries. It is often heard that sign language is "universal," but this is not true. With a few exceptions, such as Canada which uses primarily American sign language and the Philippines which does also with some modifications, other countries have their own sign systems. England, for example, uses a two-handed alphabet. Japan builds their sign system on the characters of their language, as does Korea. Through a recent survey we have learned there are four alphabets in Spanish signs and no common denominator among the South American countries. Each country has its own sign system and in Mexico signs may even change from city to city.

The deaf have devised what is called Gestuno for use at such events as the World Congress for the Deaf and the Deaf Olympic games, but there are few who are proficient in it. In future years it may prove valuable, but at this point it is far from what could be called a universal sign language.

Anyone feeling called to foreign missionary service with the deaf as their target population would have to learn the spoken language first, then the sign language from the nationals. One of the major obstacles is that some of the underdeveloped nations do not have any systematic education for the deaf, if any education at all. One of the greatest needs of which I am aware is for deaf children in underdeveloped nations to receive an education, then be presented with the gospel message.

Regarding ministry to the deaf, the following statements must be prefaced with the reason for making them. For many years I have been involved in training interpreters and ministers to the deaf. From my own experience, which has been very positive and heartwarming, I project the image of ministry to the deaf as an enjoyable calling. However, some feedback I have received from former students is that I need to warn those who plan to enter this ministry a little more explicitly.

I must caution anyone who feels inclined to minister to the deaf that it is in no way an easy ministry. Yes, there is great reward and a feeling of self-satisfaction; however, it also has its times of frustration and discouragement. It is easy to be misunderstood because of the communication modes being used. Lips can be misread, signs that have multiple meanings may cause problems, facial expressions that convey one message while the signs or lips convey another can cause hard feelings, and so on.

I find it difficult to make some comments because I do not wish to stereotype the "deaf" as always doing this or that. Those who work with the deaf discover after a time that there are certain common denominators to some behaviors due to the handicap of deafness, but I think we need to be careful not to categorize them by the actions of a few.

One legitimate characteristic I hear stated is that the deaf are "blunt." It is difficult to give nuances or changed meanings in signs. It is hard to "beat around the bush" about something you have to put in visible form, so one just has to "say" it and trust that the hearers will understand. As a result, deaf persons are accused of being blunt!

Another characteristic that I hear ministers say is that the deaf are "careful" with their money. I have occasionally noted this to be true. I will never forget how one student who came from very well-to-do parents and drove a new car refused to loan his teacher 50¢ for lunch when he forgot his lunch money! The probable reason for this frugality is that the deaf in general are not usually employed in high-wage jobs, and are accustomed to receiving everything free during their school days. (The national census of the deaf emphasized this, as covered in chapter 8 on sociology.) Realizing this, the pastor must explain the doctrine of tithing very carefully lest the deaf person feels he has to "buy" the minister's services.

Another aspect of deafness is the time element. For some reason it seems that deaf persons do not have the same consciousness of time as do the hearing. This can be illustrated by the fact that as a hearing person you could be blindfolded but allowed to hear the normal sounds of the day and you could still almost tell the time of day by the sounds you hear—a plane passing overhead on a regular basis, a train whistle, birds singing, traffic sounds, and so on. The deaf are deprived of this and do not seem to notice the passage of time. They may visit you and stay much later than you are accustomed to entertaining guests. If this occurs, politely excuse yourself and inform your guests that you must retire so as to be at your best for the next day's activities.

If there is any one thing that will destroy a person's ministry it is failure to keep confidences that are revealed during the counseling session. The minister must be aware that the deaf community is a very closely entwined group. What is related to him should not be discussed with others lest it destroy his relationship and benefit to the counselee. The deaf are very reluctant to discuss some matters because they are not sure what they say will remain with the minister. This is very sad indeed!

The deaf may need to be taught the meaning and purpose of worship. Try to ascertain how much they actually comprehend. They will want to learn how to worship and you must instruct them both by teaching and example. Sometimes the deaf feel freer to worship at the altar after the service where they can feel alone with God and not under any group pressure.

Worship services with the deaf are very different in tone and feeling. If you have not been exposed to many of these types of worship services, you may feel uncomfortable at first. The song service may have instrumental accompaniment or it may not. Some deaf persons may use their voices with little quality; others may make no sound at all. Assure them that the sound of their voice is pleasing to God and is not personally offensive to the hearing. (If in a service with the hearing it is better that they not use their voices.) The leader may be deaf and have a distorted sense of rhythm and hence the songs may not inspire you too much.

Praying with the eyes open always seems strange at first, but if you think about it there is no other way for public prayer except to watch the person praying in signs or with his lips. The person who is doing the praying keeps his eyes closed and head bowed while all the other parishioners watch.

Special songs may or may not be on key. Remember the deaf are receiving their inspiration from what is signed and the message of it and only partially from the rhythm. A piano is a great help to the hearing leader in keeping time with the music, and the hard-of-hearing enjoy the music. It may also assist a hard-of-hearing songleader.

Sermons that have the outline on a chalkboard in front of you may be disturbing at first but they really help the deaf follow what is being preached. The main thing to remember is that the service is for the deaf, not the hearing. After a while, you will feel comfortable with their type of worship. Separate services afford the deaf an opportunity to participate in the worship service itself. Interpreted services make the deaf feel somewhat like spectators.

3

Physical Plant for a Deaf Church

When a pastor or church is approached about starting a deaf ministry the first thought is, "Where can we locate it? What room is not being used during the church educational hour?" Not strange then is the fact that we find deaf congregations in places such as church kitchens, parsonages, stairwells, and even storage rooms!

More will be said later about starting a deaf ministry in a local church, but let me emphasize that physical facilities must come into prominent focus in the initial considerations.

One must remember deaf persons use their *eyes* as substitutes for their *ears*. Communicating in the language of signs for any length of time becomes very tiring to anyone, to say nothing of the deaf themselves who are in silence as well! Bearing this in mind, the thoughtful, truly concerned, and understanding church provides facilities that will reduce the handicap, not increase it!

Let us begin by considering the room itself. It should be comfortable in size so the beginning deaf group will not feel "lost in the huge auditorium" or that they have no room to move. Since drowsiness occurs in silence, poor ventilation, and dimly lit rooms, both ventilation and good lighting need to be available. Indirect nonglaring lighting should be provided. The best lighting should be above the speaker, not above the congregation, and it should not be glaring or directly in their eyes.

Another element of a deaf church is the arrangement of platform facilities. A background wall should be of such a color as to offer a contrast to the speaker. Many churches use a large span of pastel draperies behind which a chalkboard can be hung for an easily accessible visual aid (a necessity in a deaf church).

The podium or pulpit must not be higher than the speaker's waist so as to enable the deaf to see the signs easily and clearly.

Some churches also provide flannelboards and overhead projectors. Remember, everything possible must be done to communicate with the deaf.

A word must be said here about the location of the room(s) for the use of the deaf. Although the deaf have various levels of hearing loss, there are few that are, as hearing people sometimes say, "stone deaf"; therefore, if the deaf church is located near a children's church, nursery, or other such activities hearing aids will "pick up" and amplify these background noises and distract from the church service. Remember, those who are hearing-impaired are trying to receive everything they can.

A final consideration should be the room or chapel itself. Carpeting and semicircle pews or chairs are ideal. A piano is helpful and a blessing to those who can hear even at a reduced level.

One should not look at these suggestions with the attitude, "The deaf expect too much, we can't afford it." I have found that not to be the case. The deaf are highly appreciative of any and all provisions and facilities that are afforded them. This information is given for those who need instruction in what is needed to make the worship experience the most meaningful for the deaf.

One can begin on a very simple level and progress toward ideal facilities. A pastor will soon learn the deaf will "pitch in" and help do most of the work and even provide the finances. The deaf are a joy to have in the church!

4

Educational Needs for Ministry to the Deaf

Of primary concern in any educational situation is curriculum. For the hearing church the superintendent simply orders the appropriate age-level materials and correlated visual aids. The teacher has the instructor's manual; the pupil has a quarterly and sometimes a workbook. No attention needs to be given to language level for that comes inherently with the materials. Not so with the deaf.

One must first be aware of the language level of the average deaf person. In 1965 the Babbidge Report[4] revealed that the *mean* reading level for a graduate of the residential deaf schools in the U.S. was fourth grade. Studies are being made by various systems of Total Communication to raise that, but nothing significant appears to have been accomplished yet. This simply means that 50 percent of the deaf have *less than* a fourth-grade reading level. Assuming the average local church does not consist of deaf college students, we must then assume by random sample that 50 percent of a deaf congregation must be taught at that level or above. The deaf can understand clearly the message of the gospel if a simple vocabulary is used. The use of complicated synonyms for simple terms needs to be avoided. For example, you could say we had an *exhilarating* time at the picnic, and someone might not understand. The word *exciting* would be more easily understood.

A second consideration is that when educating anyone we must go from the *known* to the unknown. Biblical knowledge may be very limited for a deaf person attending worship services for the first time. Realizing also that learning occurs by going from the concrete to the abstract, religious terms such as faith, salvation, trinity, redemption, etc. complicate the situation. The materials used in this educational process must be tailored to the audience.

After admitting the above, it would seem a simple task to leaf through a publisher's catalog and select the required materials. Not so. There are definitely limited sources and subject titles.[5] Upon selection of what is considered a basic quarterly tool one may find that an instructor's manual is not available—nor is a workbook! The instructor's manual prepared for hearing persons merely expands the textual materials and increases the amount of context, of which you already have more than sufficient.

Visual aids, as already alluded to, are important to a deaf person's comprehension. Next problem? None are made to correlate with the lessons. You must devise your own materials! The skills and creativity of the individual teacher will determine how successful he is with this project.

One must determine how many age-level and, subsequently, language-level classes are needed. After deciding on curriculum and materials, one must find teachers and classroom space for each level, which may tax the facilities provided. Also necessary is the proper equipment to accomplish the teacher's goals.

An overhead projector is an excellent tool to use with the deaf, since you can prepare your materials prior to class time and face the class while they are viewing it. It is effective to have transparencies with verses printed on them that you wish to emphasize in the lesson. A chalkboard is also helpful to illustrate or diagram aspects of the lesson. A flannelgraph is a fine tool, especially to tell stories to deaf children. However, unless you have a rotating library of flannelgraph materials, the cost can become prohibitive. An innovative teacher preparing his own materials can overcome this obstacle.

In conclusion, a word needs to be said about various alternatives regarding the deaf who are orally or visually impaired. If the deaf are oral, or if some are oral and others use Total Communication, this must be taken into consideration. The oral deaf need to be seated where they can, as much as possible, have a frontal view of the teacher. Since the student will need to lipread, the teacher must remember to always face the class when speaking. He must not speak too rapidly or exaggerate his lip movements. To do so makes lipreading impossible. If the teacher signs and speaks he or she should sign to the side of the mouth. The overhead projector or chalkboard would be of great assistance in comprehension.

If some are visually impaired, the lighting should be arranged so they can make use of all the vision they have. This does not always mean having a bright light on the teacher. A nonglaring medium light source may be used. It would be well to ask these students under which conditions they can see the best. Distance from the teacher is also a consideration needing attention.

In a church where an interpreter must be used in lieu of a regular teacher, the interpreter's clothing should be pastel-colored without floral, checkered, or plaid designs. A contrasting background is ideal.

Integrating the deaf with the hearing class should be discouraged and done only when absolutely necessary. The deaf need instruction on their own language level using their mode of communication, and ignoring this will cause the deaf group to deteriorate rapidly. The only exception to this would be if all the hearing children in the class can communicate with the deaf children and discussion can be conducted in Total Communication. I know of only rare situations where this is done.

5

Administrative Concerns of Ministry to the Deaf

A pastor (minister) is the primary administrator of any local church, whether he desires it or not. Having pastored myself I can see a definite need for information regarding specific tangible and intangible, foreseen and unforeseen circumstances as relates to a deaf group.

As mentioned previously, the first concern of the pastor is "space" for a deaf group. Many times the sequence of priorities is as follows: space, equipment, educational materials, an interpreter or minister to the deaf. If the latter initiates the group, the sequence recedes to space, equipment, and educational materials.

More often than not, as the number of deaf constituents increases so do misunderstandings and injured feelings. The pastor "never dreamed" the deaf would need "more or a better" space. Nor did he think the deaf would want their offerings separate from the hearing church; nor that they would like a "full-time" minister; nor that they would not feel obligated to "pay rent" on their deaf chapel or help pay for heat, lights, water, custodial services, etc.! And the deaf "never dreamed" the hearing church did not want them to use the printing equipment or any supplies without special permission, or that they had to "reserve" the kitchen for Saturday night!

Such problems do arise, especially if the hearing church overextends itself financially and attempts to extract finances from every group within the church. The discussion that follows should help eliminate such misunderstandings.

The key word for the pastor/administrator is *communication.* Never "assume" the deaf understand unless you have carefully explained it to them through an interpreter. Admittedly, even the hearing interpreter may misunderstand occasionally but be sure you do all you can to eliminate this.

Open and total communication will reduce many misunderstandings between the deaf and hearing. We must look at the deaf/hearing relationship both initially and in the future because as the group increases and changes, the relationship becomes more complex. An interpreter or a part- or full-time minister to the deaf resolves many problems since he acts as liaison and go-between for the pastor.

Initially, the hearing congregation is thrilled with the thought that the deaf are receiving the gospel through an interpreter or worker. The "distraction" of the interpreter fades as it becomes a common sight. It may be disturbing to find that they must sit near the front but even that is easily ignored—since churches generally fill back to front anyway.

Let us assume now that the group which began as two or three persons now averages 15 in attendance. They decide they would like to have separate services from the hearing congregation. The congregation would rather they did not. The pastor considers such a move as a "split" in his church—and the battle is on! I say this only to illustrate how simply all this could have been avoided by sitting down with the church ruling body—the board, trustees, or elders—and writing down the present and future goals and guidelines. Church approval in writing eliminates future misunderstandings with future pastors or administrators.

Congregations that want a ministry to the deaf in their church should consider it as a missions outreach and provide space and utilities free of charge. Later on, after the group increases, they should let the deaf decide if they wish to contribute finances for this purpose.

From its inception, the church should strive to have at least a part-time, if not full-time, salaried minister to the deaf. If the hearing church must use a volunteer worker, contacts should be made through the district organization to raise support to change this situation as soon as possible.

Years ago a bank president told my wife as a new employee—"When it comes to money, don't trust anyone!" When it comes to finances in the church be sure everything is open and honest. Some deaf churches have combined accounts with the hearing church, which in turn disburses all funds and, if insufficient, subsidizes the deaf fund from general funds. This appears to work well but gives the deaf the sense of giving to no one in particular and makes "giving" impersonal rather than a spiritual part of worship. When they know it is going to their faithful, patient, gracious minister whom they love it helps them feel a part of the ministry.

If completely separate accounts are established all monies should be counted by at least two persons (deacons or board members), a record initialed, and then deposited in a local bank. All checks should be signed by two persons (ideally, the pastor and the treasurer). This solves two problems. First, the pastor knows exactly where the money is spent. Second, no accusations can be made as to disbursements. By having a separate account the treasurer of the hearing church has less bookkeeping and if later the deaf group begins their own services it eliminates a great deal of confusion.

Along with having separate funds, the possibility of having a separate board should be considered. If attached to a hearing church, having a separate board or committee as consultants to the hearing board would be well appreciated by those unknowledgeable about the deaf. However, if the church and funds are separate it facilitates matters to have a separate board for administrative purposes. It should be emphasized: any deaf church that uses the facilities of a hearing church must be amenable and acquiescent to the decisions of the board of that church. If the decisions of such a board (and I consider this rare) are totally unacceptable to the deaf group, then a change of facilities appears in order. This should not be construed as a "split," but rather like a child leaving home to establish his own family and residence.

One of the primary advantages of a deaf church being attached to a hearing church is that the hearing children of deaf parents may attend similarly timed church functions, thus receiving instruction in classes for their age-level. This also frees the deaf members to benefit as much as possible from their class without disciplinary distractions.

Where deaf churches are separate, some bus their

children to a nearby hearing church of the same affiliation.

A general rule of thumb is for larger metropolitan areas with sizable deaf populations to establish separate independent congregations while urban and more rural areas would remain attached to hearing churches. The latter are more accustomed to fellowship and social interchange with hearing people because of the lower deaf population.

A critical relationship too often taken for granted is that between the pastor of the hearing church (usually not knowledgeable about the deaf) and the pastor, interpreter, or worker of the deaf church. If the latter is a lay person the hearing pastor may feel uneasy about sharing openly with him and must be discretionary in his relationships. However, by virtue of the deaf worker's position, the pastor should respect and be amenable to him in areas of concern about which he may be ignorant. If the minister to the deaf is a credentialed, licensed, or ordained minister of the gospel, he should be looked upon as an "associate" or co-pastor and given full administrative authority to deal with any and all situations in consultation with the senior pastor.

If the pastor to the deaf and his wife are both deaf, the ideal situation would be for the church to have an interpreter to function alongside the deaf pastor in his relations with the hearing pastor and with the community. Such an interpreter adds greatly to the effectiveness of deaf ministry in the church.

Some other advantages to the combination of the deaf and hearing church are as follows: the congregation sees the need of the deaf, the facilities are used jointly, the deaf are not isolated, the pastor of the deaf (assuming he is hearing) profits spiritually from the services, the deaf learn by observation how to worship, and forces are combined for advertising the church services.

Some disadvantages of this arrangement are: the deaf may feel uneasy and uncomfortable in a service with hearing people, they may feel they are "on display" when seated in the front with an interpreter, the hearing pastor may become jealous because he cannot communicate with the deaf, the deaf may not feel welcome and complain that the hearing people are not sufficiently friendly, and the hearing may avoid the deaf because they cannot communicate with them adequately.

If you are the pioneer pastor of the deaf, a few questions should be adequately resolved in your mind before proceeding: Are the facilities adequate for what you envision of your group? How does the hearing pastor feel toward the deaf? What do the people in the church think of having the deaf in their services? Are there many deaf in the area? Is the church having any problems or difficult circumstances that would make it an inopportune time for starting this group? How receptive is the church to the deaf?

Since most deaf churches are either attached to or mothered by a hearing church, the following are some legitimate expectations the pastor of that church may have:

1. His trust will not be betrayed.
2. What will be done with the money will be made clear.
3. Who will have what responsibility will be made clear.

4. There will be mutual respect.
5. The deaf church will maintain good communications in order to avoid conflicts for use of transportation or building facilities.
6. The deaf church will notify the hearing pastor of all activities and keep him abreast of progress and victories.
7. The deaf church will not isolate itself.

Keeping aware of the above principles and guidelines will save those who minister to the deaf from many a pitfall.

6
Psychology of Deafness for the Minister

At the outset of this chapter we must emphasize that this brief treatise regarding the psychology of deafness is in no way intended to be exhaustive or totally inclusive. It is but a general approach to make the professional or paraprofessional aware of some aspects of deafness so he or she may better improve services to this population.

I am inclined to agree that our perspective must be that there is no true "psychology of deafness," but there are aspects of this handicap we can examine while remembering the deaf are *individuals* and no two are alike. I always remind people that there is no psychology study that fits *all* deaf people anymore than we can say all hearing people exhibit specific behavior patterns.

We must define the population about which we are speaking. "The deaf" are those whose "loss of hearing is sufficiently severe to render an understanding of conversational speech impossible in most situations with or without a hearing aid."[6] It matters not whether these individuals' loss is due to genetics, an accident, an illness, or psychological reasons. If they function as deaf persons for the ordinary purposes of life they need someone to minister to them.

No hearing person can completely experience the full impact of deafness. Being put in a glass cell in the middle of a room with hearing people talking all around you is one of the best illustrations of what it means to be deaf. However, a hearing person, regardless of his attempted projection into this mode, cannot have a "total experience" of deafness.

The same thing applies to the deaf person. Depending on the onset of his hearing loss, he lacks a *total experience*, hence, his personality as well as his language and education are affected.

The normal hearing child receives auditory input from the time he is born. Although he cannot understand or repeat everything he hears he is still learning for later years. Any parent is aware that "babbling" to an infant will usually get an attempted similar response. This keeps the baby aurally in contact with his environment. Limiting this experience causes some of the behaviors observed in the deaf population.

"Smile, and the world smiles with you," is an adage that is pertinent to the deaf. Many misunderstandings result from a simple smile. The hearing person smiles and makes a statement. The deaf person, not understanding but returning the smile, nods his head. The hearing person subsequently believes he has been understood, as does the deaf person, and both depart knowing little about the interchange. Later great frustration develops on the part of both communicants.

Let us start at the beginning and look at what happens psychologically when deafness is discovered. Most parents while expecting a child pray and trust their new baby will be normal in every way. This is a natural, healthy expectation so it should not seem unusual that the parents breathe a sigh of relief after delivery when they discover the child *appears* to be normal physically. As time progresses the mother may suspect the infant does not hear at times but she generally dismisses the thought. If it is the first child the parents may not realize at what age an infant should respond, so the discovery may be later than with subsequent children.

When the discovery is finally admitted and positively diagnosed by physicians and audiologists the impact is great. The first reaction is unbelief, "No, it can't be!" This is followed by, "Why my child?" The mother feels guilty because she bore a handicapped child. The father may feel guilty because he fathered a handicapped child. They may both project that guilt by blaming their spouse, "There is no hereditary deafness in my family background!" Then the grandparents enter the scene, "Why did she/he ever marry him/her?" And so on the ripples go when the "stone" labeled "deaf" is dropped into the brook.

The parents feel grief, guilt, anger, and helplessness in this moment of truth. The natural question to ask is, "What can I do? Where can I get help?" The physician, not being an educator (although well qualified to diagnose deafness), is limited in his knowledge of what to do and where to go. The average physician usually suggests the parents go to a "speech and hearing center" in their area. The speech and hearing center many times, in an attempt to calm their fears and frustrations, assures the parents, "Your child will be able to speak and function like a *normal* child." Many such centers advocate only an oral approach and further postpone real communication to the years when the child can speak vocally. Little wonder there is a language gap of several years later on!

Recent developments in research by such professionals as Dr. McCay Vernon; Eugene O. Mindel, M.D.; Hilde Schlesinger, M.D.; and Dr. Kaye Meadows[7] have brought the method of Total Communication to the forefront, whereby parents can learn to communicate with their hearing-impaired children at the earliest moment. Total Communication is defined as:

> The right of every deaf child to use all forms of communication so that he may have the full opportunity to develop language competence at the earliest possible age. This implies introduction to a reliable, receptive-expressive symbol system in the preschool years between birth and age 5. Total Communication includes the full spectrum of language modes: child-devised gestures, the language of signs, speech, speechreading, fingerspelling, reading, and writing. Total Communication also holds that every deaf child should have the opportunity to develop any remnant of residual hearing for the enhancement of speech and speechreading skills through the use of individual and/or high-fidelity group-amplification systems.[8]

Parents of deaf children should be made aware of all opportunities of educational methods and then decide on the basis of severity of loss, facilities available, and what is best for their child now and in his future adult life. They must realize their decision will fairly well determine the child's successful adaptation to society.

The parents will never completely resolve their feelings toward their child's deafness, but confronting the issue and communicating freely with each other will greatly reduce the frustration. But frustrations will still occur. For example, when they want the child they must go *to* him if he's out of sight or not looking at them. And they cannot call him on the telephone. Yes, misunderstandings will still occur by communication breakdown and misread lips, voice, and/or signs but they can be greatly reduced.

Acceptance by peers, parents, and siblings all help reduce the psychological impact of deafness. Parents need to accept their child's deafness and do everything they can to help him overcome his handicap, rather than spending wishful years trying to pretend it does not exist.

The minister to the deaf needs to be sensitive to these aspects of the deaf. Open communication in the deaf person's mode is greatly needed for a successful ministry.

7

Physiological Aspects of Deafness

The actual physiology of deafness may not seem important to the minister but a knowledge of the simple basics will help him in counseling the deaf about their handicap.

One must also understand that when we say a person is "deaf" we may be speaking of anything from a mild loss of hearing to a severe loss. Just as we do not classify all people who wear glasses as blind, we cannot classify all who have a hearing loss as totally deaf (although they may function as deaf with a mild loss or as hard-of-hearing while having a profound loss!). You need not do the classifying as they will do so themselves.

We will not go into all the causes of deafness but we will note that there are two types—conductive and sensorineural. Conductive deafness simply means there is a problem in conducting sound through the chain of bones (see p. 49)—the hammer (malleus), anvil (incus), and stirrup (stapes). The most common cause of this kind of deafness is otosclerosis (calcification of the footplate of the stirrup), which hinders the conduction of sound to the cochlea. This type of deafness usually occurs in late adolescence or early twenties and has a high cure rate by a surgical procedure called a stapedectomy. There are other surgical procedures for correction of hearing loss but to expect medical miracle cures for the profoundly deaf is an effort in futility.

The second type of deafness is sensorineural, for which there is at present no correction or cure. This means that the lesion or defect is within the inner ear, usually the eighth nerve, which carries the sound to the cortex of the brain. It is so deep within the skull that to attempt to correct this would destroy more tissue than it would correct. Newspaper ads that purport to offer a "cure" for such deafness are misleading.

A word needs to be said here about the hearing aids the hard-of-hearing use. Many hearing persons think that if a deaf person has a hearing aid he can "hear" and understand normal conversation. This is not true. A hearing aid is merely an amplification system to supplement what residual hearing the person has. If he hears speech as a garbled mass of noise, to increase that sound will not result in comprehension. It will only make that garbled mass of noise louder and possibly painful! Deaf persons with hearing aids try to avoid exposure to loud sounds unless they have the opportunity to turn off the hearing aid.

As a minister you may notice that someone's hearing aid is howling or producing a high-pitched shrill sound. It is not considered impolite to tell the deaf person about it. On the contrary, he will appreciate your help.

Although the minister may never have to evaluate audiograms, a knowledge of what a person can hear at specific levels is helpful to understanding the deaf person.

ANATOMY OF THE EAR

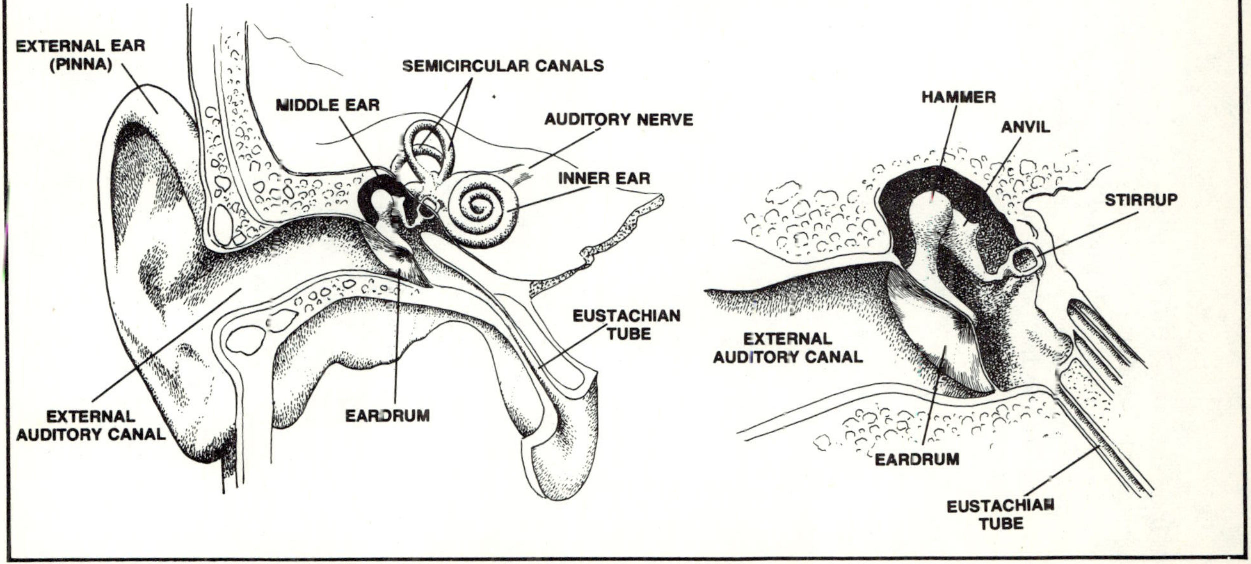

It must be noted that for unknown reasons there are occasionally deaf people with a profound loss who function like those with a mild loss; and the opposite is also true. This may only prove that our testing mechanisms are not perfect, or at least less than we would sometimes prefer.

8

Sociological Aspects of Deafness

There are some sociological aspects of the deaf population that need highlighting for the minister. The following is based on surveys and research and is in no way intended to bias or discriminate against the deaf.

First, one must be aware that the deaf are a *subculture.* This means they have a culture of their own within the societal structure of the community. This does not mean they have no contact with the larger hearing community, but after work and in their leisure time they tend to have social interaction primarily with "their own kind," i.e. other deaf. This is brought about not by design but by such factors as a common background. They attend deaf school or classes together and remain friends after graduation. If they attend college the majority go to Gallaudet College, Washington, D.C., the only liberal arts college for the deaf in the world. If they attend other colleges, the same applies- they are there because other deaf students are there!

The deaf find their social life easier with other deaf because of the ease of communication and commonality of handicap. It is more difficult for the deaf to have meaningful social relationships with hearing people unless both can communicate fluently in the same communication mode, whether orally, with Total Communication, or whatever.

They date and later marry another deaf person (86 percent of all deaf prefer to marry a deaf spouse) who also has deaf friends. So the process tends to ingrow itself. Social activities usually extend to deaf clubs, religious services, or team sports, etc.—again primarily deaf-oriented.

There are some other trends that are supported by statistics from "The Deaf Population of the U.S."[9] One of these is that the deaf normally court for a longer time than hearing persons (anywhere from 3 to 7 years) and they marry later. By age 34 less than six in ten deaf are married while almost eight in ten hearing people are married. We might think the later marriage would lower the divorce rate but this does not seem to be true. The deaf divorce rate is 3.8 percent as compared to the hearing, 3.6 percent. The divorce rate among deaf who marry hearing spouses is far higher.

The fact deaf persons marry later in life may also be due to their extended formal education and the reluctance of their parents to permit them to become self-reliant individuals. It is not uncommon for parents of deaf young people to delay driving a car even to their mid-twenties.

One of the questions asked most often is, "Should the deaf person marry a hearing mate?" I believe this is a valid question and should be considered in detail. I must preface my remarks by saying I am not opposed to deaf and hearing persons marrying, *if*. . . . Too often I am misquoted and misunderstood as saying I do not approve of deaf and hearing persons marrying each other. The "if" is what needs to be considered.

If both parties consider all the aspects of the question—and are willing to face them for a lifetime and still wish to proceed with the marriage—I give my approval.

Let us consider the problems apart from what Christian principles can do to solve disagreements. Our first consideration will assume the husband is deaf and marries a hearing woman. The wife becomes, by virtue of position and duty, a full-time, 24-hour-a-day interpreter for her husband. Although the husband is the head of the house, he must rely on his wife to: (1) answer the phone and interpret the conversations (some deaf have TTY'S for phone communication with each other); (2) answer the door when it is a hearing person who cannot communicate; and (3) either make decisions or interpret business decisions. This is further complicated with the arrival of children who also need her to interpret until they can communicate using their father's mode (whatever that may be). I cannot help but believe it is very difficult to be in this role, as a wife, and not overstep lines of authority in the home or just plain eclipse the husband's role in the family.

Now let us reverse the roles—the husband hearing, the wife deaf. Now the husband can exert his authority as the head of the house, but he tends to do so more easily by not explaining business matters to his wife. If he does involve her, he becomes the lifetime interpreter! If he doesn't, she feels left out. Now the father can communicate with his children and discipline them, however, he is away from the home the major part of the day. His wife may not be aware of what has transpired during the day. Now it is the husband who must take time to communicate phone messages, business deals, etc.

Obviously there are some common problems as well. Suspicions arise even between two hearing persons. A marriage would surely be greatly tested regarding "trust" when you could not hear your mate's conversations with others.

The entertainment problem surfaces quickly. The deaf spouse may like active sports that need little verbal involvement, while the other may like drama, theater, and concerts. The deaf spouse cannot feel completely at ease with all hearing people, nor does the hearing person feel comfortable with all deaf persons at a social gathering. Such feelings tend to break down the unity between a couple and could become a large wedge in dividing the home.

Most deaf communities have a deaf club whose makeup varies geographically. Attendance by the hearing spouse could become a burden.

I was once approached by a young lady who intended to marry a deaf man. In the course of the conversation she mentioned that after marriage they would have no phone, TV, or radio. I asked, "Why not?" She replied, "Since my husband cannot enjoy them, it would not be fair for me to do so!" I advised against such a mistake. Hearing people are psychologically "hearing" and depend on auditory stimulation to retain normal homeostasis or equilibrium. A marriage that forces the other to become what he is not will not long survive.

Now back to our original question: "Should the deaf and hearing marry?" This is an individual matter that cannot be answered by "yes" or "no." For those who consider the above problems and openly and honestly feel they can make their marriage a success by "love conquering all," then I say, "Go ahead." But if they have candid reservations or have reacted by saying, "I never thought of that," then maybe they should reconsider.

I am not an authority on deaf-hearing marriages but I strongly suspect that some who are not happy have not come to the place they would admit it to anyone. (This is probably true of many hearing marriages as well.) The higher divorce rate should also be an indicator for decisionmaking.

This subculture of the "silent minority" has been neglected and overlooked for centuries. Why else is deaf education only 150 years old while normal hearing education is thousands of years old? Why else are they underemployed or unemployed, or passed up for promotions and increased wages? Why else are there so few religious services available to them? Why else has TV until recently not been captioned? It is because their handicap is not visible. No one *notices* until they confront the communication barrier and see someone signing or writing notes. Then they become concerned because they find themselves handicapped in communication! Mr. Minister, are you concerned?

While on the subject of the discrimination of the deaf we can again consult the deaf census: "While employment is not as high among the deaf population as would be desirable, it does not arouse as much concern as underemployment—employment in positions incompatible with the workers' intelligence, skills, and education."

Williams and Sussman (1971) in discussing the employment picture state:

> This glowing picture nonetheless has three serious flaws. The first is that employed deaf people are very often seriously underemployed. The deaf college graduate linotype-operator pressman is quite common, for example. Everywhere we find deaf men and women of normal or above average abilities operating automatic machines, performing simple assembly line operations, or otherwise occupied in unchallenging routines. This stereotyping illustrates the inadvertent discriminatory attitudes toward deaf job applicants that are inevitable among slightly informed professionals when relating with this or another small minority that has very complex characteristics.

An official in the U.S. Department of Labor expressed a similar viewpoint:

> In an economy where the rate of unemployment is one of the lowest in modern history and *the* lowest in over 15 years, where over a million and a half additional workers are absorbed every year in our labor market, the deaf should find employment quite readily—but too often it is at a level greatly below their true capacities. They quickly reach a plateau, and there they remain. As a result, underemployment is so prevalent as to become a major problem for most deaf people who are capable and interested in working (Stahler, 1969).

Although these figures are from several years past, there has been no upsurge of interest to hire the deaf in recent years. It is true we are seeing more deaf adults in administrative positions and in our school systems, but the number is still very meager in contrast to the hearing person's opportunities. This is brought to light by the fact that ". . . almost 43 percent of deaf adults who have completed 13 years or more of school (i.e., have one or more years of higher education) have principal occupations in the following categories: clerical, transit and nontransit operatives, farm and nonfarm laborers, and service and household workers. Underemployment certainly describes many of these job placements, though not necessarily all."[10]

The deaf have been overlooked and neglected primarily because their handicap is not visible. I do not have any suggestions for a symbol for the handicapped in the U.S., but I feel it is unfortunate that the symbol is a wheelchair! Great strides are being made to build ramps in government buildings to aid the wheelchair victim but the same offices ignore the deaf as job applicants. The ignorance of the general public about the problems of deafness is appalling. No one notices the deaf until they confront the communication barrier themselves. Then they become concerned because they find themselves *handicapped* in communication!

Mr. Minister . . . are you concerned!

9

Insights Into the Education of the Deaf

The minister to a hearing church would rarely be concerned with the educational background and process of public education of his parishioners. Primarily, this is because he probably came through the same process himself. This is not true of those who are hearing and minister to the deaf. A basic knowledge of what they have gone through helps one to communicate with them on their level.

The education of the deaf infant born to hearing parents can take several directions. If the parents choose an *oral only* approach hopefully they will enroll their child in a program as early as 18 months. The process of teaching the child is very slow.

Dr. Edgar Lowell, administrator of the famed John Tracy Clinic in Los Angeles, California, states that it takes 10,000 repetitions of a word before the child can conceptualize the word. This does not mean he can speak it yet—only understand that what he "saw" on the lips is, e.g., "shoe." This may take as long as a year. Assuming the child was 18 months when enrolled, at 30 months he has a one-word vocabulary. Probably later words would come more easily so let us say the child has a 200-word vocabulary at age 5. What is that when compared to a hearing child's vocabulary of several thousand words? But let us not belittle these efforts. There are fantastic products of such programs in the world today (although too few).

Now let us hypothesize that the deaf infant has deaf parents who communicate using the language of signs. He may or may not go to a preschool program for deaf children but from the earliest age he *communicates* with his parents. He enters school better socially adjusted, more self-confident, and with at least a symbol system of language. Now formal education begins in either a day-school program or a state residential school for the deaf. If the latter, this means an abrupt, incomprehensible separation from family, friends, and familiar surroundings, but a definitely necessary step in life.

In the first year the child may learn about 50 nouns and 12 verbs. By the end of the second year, even if this is increased to a 300-word vocabulary, the child is now 7 years old! The language gap is there and gets increasingly wider as his hearing peers bound ahead, until at graduation (age 18-20) the average deaf graduate from a residential school in the U.S. has an equivalent eighth-grade education with a fourth-grade reading level![11]

Keeping this in mind, it is little wonder that few can cope with post-secondary school academics. Realizing this will help the minister in both his preaching and teaching responsibilities.

One of the problems of preaching or teaching in a deaf church is that you have people of various vocabulary and comprehension levels. The same is true of hearing congregations but we are not so conscious of it. We do not always know when our message did not get through. The deaf are eager to learn and many times visibly react through facial expressions to let you know they did not understand the word you used or the concept you are trying to convey. For this reason the minister needs to be very discerning of his congregation as he preaches or teaches. The multiplied use of various visual aids will help overcome this barrier.

Just as an elementary or secondary school is graded into ability groupings so should be the religious program in a deaf church. The sole difference is in a deaf church you can grade only by the availability of personnel. When setting up classes be careful not to establish "reputations" or levels of classes, such as one being the "low nonverbal" class, the second "more verbal," and the third "highly verbal." The deaf will naturally attend the class where they comprehend the most. Class names like "Kings Men," "Searchers for Truth," etc. give no connotation of language levels and accomplish the same thing.

When beginning a deaf class in a newly organized church or group, one is faced with the question, "What should I teach?" This is complicated by the fact that all the deaf of a wide spectrum of ages are in the one class.

A good place to begin is with simple Biblical truths such as Creation, sin, salvation, the Bible, and the life of Jesus. As time progresses, and the class grows and divides into other classes, such themes can be broken down into smaller segments, such as the Trinity, the Ten Commandments, and the miracles of Jesus, without being obviously repetitious. Never forget: Repetition is the key to education. We move from the known to the unknown, so background and basic knowledge is essential to understanding new material.

The religious education program in the deaf church must include a Bible-study session. Whether it is held on a weeknight, weekday mornings, or any other convenient time it should be a Bible study with discussion, questions, and answers. The deaf enjoy it and profit greatly from these times of fellowship around the Word of God.

When the deaf church grows to where it can train its own Sunday school teachers a class should be established to train them. Materials are available through most denominational headquarters, but remember they will need to be adapted for deaf audiences.

Last, but definitely not least, education in evangelism methods should be undertaken. The deaf should be given instruction in how to evangelize.

10

Developing a Deaf Ministry

"How do I begin?" This agelong question has been asked by countless people anxious to provide religious services for the deaf. What is disconcerting is that many times these same people have had all kinds of preparation—training in signs, psychology of deafness, interpreting, reverse interpreting, how to teach and preach to the deaf. But when they are out there in a strange city and they have to know which way to proceed all the academia does not seem to help.

During the Korean War I completed basic training and was ordered to Korea. A friend asked, "Are you prepared to go to war?" I answered, "No!" But when I arrived there I discovered I had all the basics I needed; I just needed to apply them. The same is true with deaf ministry. You only need to apply those skills already learned.

The answer to, "How do I begin?" can vary from individual to individual and depends on the community, opportunities, employment, the potential of deaf adherents, and personal innovativeness and resourcefulness.

A new church or group of any kind is not easily begun. Deaf churches are not so much begun as they are spontaneously *erupted* into being. It seems there suddenly appears a nucleus of deaf persons who desire a spiritual leader to teach and preach to them. These become the founding stones of the church. You may be called to come and help them. The rest is *not* easy!

The most practical way for such a group to exist is to become affiliated with an already established hearing church. Many churches are happy to provide facilities for such a group. This quickly provides, for the moment at least, a meeting place, utilities, and a source for ordering supplies. As the group grows, it may have to consider a larger meeting place or build a separate deaf chapel. Some groups disassociate with the hearing church and establish their own sovereign church independent from the hearing church. I believe there is no dogmatic rule as to which way is best. It depends on the specific situation and the community. What works best for your group is the best!

In determining which hearing church would like to provide facilities for a deaf group, it is wise to start at the district level with the district director of deaf ministries. He may refer you to the sectional or lower level in your organization. The latter person may then poll the ministers of the area as to who would want to open their doors for this ministry. If there are several opportunities, then consideration should be given as to which church would be the best for the deaf. The other churches may be viewed as potential outstations for ministry to the deaf in the future. It would be wise to visit the different churches personally before making a decision.

The sectional churches could raise the support for the minister to the deaf as a missionary outreach and, thus, give the minister free course to "build the church." Admittedly, it takes magnanimous pastors and congregations to financially support a ministry in a neighboring church. This is particularly important since the deaf must be contacted individually by the minister because they cannot be appealed to by telephone, radio, or TV. When the deaf discover the minister can communicate with them in the language of signs they will become excited. In smaller communities the loneliness of the deaf and their desire and need for fellowship can be an aid in ministering to them. Acceptance in the larger metropolitan areas comes more slowly.

As explained in chapter 8, the deaf are a subculture. Because of this the best contacts for prospective members come from the deaf. Obtaining lists of addresses of deaf persons within the community is almost impossible since this is privileged information and not for public distribution. This is for the protection of the deaf because they have been exploited in the past. Other possible lists of contacts may be obtained through the state association of the N.A.D. (National Association of the Deaf). Visiting a reputable deaf club or placing posters in their meeting room is also advantageous. If affiliated with a hearing church, cards can be distributed to the congregation asking for names and addresses of any deaf they may know in their neighborhood.

When laying the groundwork for the opening services with the deaf, a projected and promoted date of beginning will help to build enthusiasm for the deaf. If special services can be arranged with a time of fellowship and/or dinner following it is a good idea to do so. The deaf are somewhat limited in their opportunities for fellowship so they find these times very refreshing and may even be reluctant to leave. The better acquainted you become with the deaf on their initial visits the greater the likelihood of their returning.

If you have a nucleus of deaf persons you will find that their friends, also deaf, will be contacted. When considering potential deaf constituents in the community you can figure two deaf per thousand hearing persons. Large industrial communities have a higher population of deaf. According to "The Deaf Population of the United States," the largest prevalence rate for prevocational deafness (19 years or older) is found in the North Central region[12] and the lowest in the Northeast,[13] the former having a rate almost 29 percent larger than the latter.

Founding churches in cities where the residential schools for the deaf are located is a good idea because many parents move to those communities so their child can be a day student rather than a residential one.

Good public relations with the various agencies serving the deaf in the community is prudent and may also result in contacts for your church.

Beginning a church has some definite benefits for the pastor. First, you are not following a predecessor, therefore, the deaf have no one with whom to constantly compare you. Second, deaf ministry is a teaching ministry. Many deaf are non-Christian with no church background or experience and you will have the benefit of teaching them many Biblical truths for the first time. And third, you have the privilege of seeing the group grow in numbers as well as spiritually and socially.

Now let us turn to the issue of interpreted services versus separate services for the deaf. Initially, when the group consists of only a few persons, interpreting the worship services is best so the deaf will feel part of a large group rather than so few. A separate Sunday school class will give you the opportunity to teach them at their language level and help you become acquainted with them personally. After the group grows to eight or ten you might consider a separate service on Sunday evening while still joining the hearing congregation during the morning service. When the group exceeds 20 they will probably desire and request separate services for both services.

It is important for the deaf and hearing to occasionally (at least once a month) meet together so the hearing congregation can see the progress of this group for which they have opened their doors, hearts, and billfolds. There is also the feeling the deaf get when they find they are a living, integral part of the larger congregation, loved and respected by them just like anyone else. The pastor of a hearing church who opposes having separate services may find he has alienated himself toward the deaf in the guise of avoiding a "split" in his church. Actually, dividing for separate services is no more of a split than dividing into various Sunday school classes.

It bears noting here that if the services are interpreted the person doing the interpreting should wear plain, pastel-colored clothing and be clean and neat at all times. Excessive jewelry, makeup, or brilliant colors are very difficult for the deaf to read signs against. Moderation should be practiced. Women must be careful for obvious reasons if they are called to interpret from a raised platform.

I prefer to have the interpreter seated between the pulpit and the deaf for whom he is interpreting. The deaf should be seated near the front of the church. In this way they can see the expressions and actions of the minister and still observe what is being said. The oral deaf can also lipread more easily. When the interpreter stands he is very distracting to the hearing. Although sign language is beautiful and many are impressed by it, at no time should the interpreter "show off" or attempt to bring attention to himself. The interpreter should at all times be as unobtrusive as possible.

Should special lighting effects be used in the hearing church in which you are interpreting a blue light may be used to illuminate the interpreter and not destroy the effects of the special presentation. Since interpreting church services will ultimately result in calls to interpret elsewhere a word needs to be said regarding this task. It is perfectly acceptable to go with the person the first time he has an encounter where he needs you. However, subsequent visits may not require your presence and you must evaluate the situation. Be careful that you do not become paternalistic in your attitude toward them so they depend on you unnecessarily.

Now at this juncture we must assume the church is in operation and we will look at the governing mechanism or operation of the church.

Depending on the type of church government that is used, the following suggestions can be altered to fit the situation. In the beginning when the deaf church is affiliated with the hearing church, the board of that church could act as the official board in consultation with the minister to the deaf until the deaf church has its own governing board. Since ministry to the deaf is a unique ministry, the minister would have to orient the board about any necessary special considerations.

As the church grows and develops responsible lay leadership, a board or committee of deaf members could take care of most matters. Such committee members could be delegated responsibilities such as treasurer, head usher, music director or song leader, social chairman (person), or any other position necessary. This committee could act as an advisory board to the board of the hearing church if necessary, but working with two different boards can be clumsy and inefficient. There is no reason the deaf should not administer their own church. They surely are more cognizant of the problems and solutions than the board of the hearing church.

11

Religious Education Ministry to the Deaf

As discussed in chapter 4, special equipment is required for meeting the needs of the educational program for the deaf. We will not reiterate that discussion but assume the church has provided the minimum equipment necessary.

In beginning the deaf church it is almost a necessity to start with only one Sunday school class. As the group increases and more personnel become available, it could divide into two groups (possibly based on age). As the church continues to grow they could further divide until it becomes feasible for them to divide according to comprehension level (as suggested in chapter 9).

The next educational concern of the deaf church would be for the children of the deaf. Generally speaking, unless a deaf couple is genetically deaf they will bear hearing children. These can be integrated into the hearing church. But the deaf children (of hearing or deaf parents) must have special consideration if you intend to present any religious training to them. Among the deaf children there may be a variety of hearing-loss levels, language skills, and/or comprehension levels. Some children may be exclusively oral while others may communicate in signs quite proficiently.

The availability of teachers and aides is an important criterion for the establishment of these classes. It should also be noted that those who teach and assist need to be aware of the special needs of these children. The class period should *not* deteriorate to "play time" but be used for constructive teaching. The rule of thumb would be to aim at simple concepts, usually 4 years below what a hearing child would understand. As the teacher becomes more acquainted with the children he/she will know at what level to teach.

Teaching deaf children can be a very rewarding experience. They crave to be understood and desire communication. Teenagers may be reluctant to accept you at first but patience, love, and communication is the key. When they discover you really do love them and are concerned about them they will take you into their confidence. Showing interest in what they do outside of church (at school and at home) will mean a great deal to them. If you are near their school, attend their sports activities. They will appreciate this and you will understand their world better.

Here are some basic principles to guide you in teaching deaf children:

1. Have sincere and unfeigned love for the children. The deaf are very discerning and will detect insincerity.

2. Maintain order and discipline in class.

3. Teach basic Christian themes such as God, Jesus, salvation, heaven, and stories of Old and New Testament characters.

In the beginning teach very simple concepts (such as God, man, Jesus, Creation). Be sure to introduce stories about Jesus chronologically, from His birth to the Cross. If you mix up the order of these events it will be confusing to the children. Teach what the Bible is. Teach words.

4. Communicate your stories with a lot of *action*. If you can't do this, then learn how to do it. Act like a child with them and play with them. Small children do not have a very large vocabulary of signs. Pantomime and action will get the message across to them. Also use a lot of facial expression.

5. Use a variety of color and colorful objects in teaching your lesson.

There are also some basic "don'ts" to guide you in teaching children:

1. Do not repeatedly use the "happy family life" theme in teaching. Many of the children attend a residential school for the deaf and the concept of the home life is incongruous with their life.

2. Do not dwell on a lot of details in a story. They are extraneous and may be confusing. Keep the story simple.

3. Do not use complex or involved signs. The children know simple signs and gestures. If you must teach them a sign for a lesson keep it simple.

4. Do not permit sporadic attendance to discourage you. Many of the children may come from non-Christian homes where their faithful attendance is neither required nor encouraged.

5. If you are emotionally upset because of discipline matters or other situations do not let it show to the children. This would upset them and increase your classroom problems.

6. Do not overreact to profane or dirty signs. The children come from a secular community and until

they are taught the difference they will continue to use them.

In addition to these basic rules there are also some general factors to keep in mind.

Have sufficient floor space and tables. When using rectangular tables sit in the middle so you can assist all the children as they need it. Semicircular tables with the teacher sitting in the center is ideal for this type of situation.

When using pictures or visual aids use them repeatedly for several lessons until they become familiar and the lesson is learned. Remember, repetition is the key to education. Keep the atmosphere alive and whenever possible involve the children themselves.

Using charts with the students' names written in large letters with stars or other stickers for lessons completed, memory work, or attendance is an excellent idea. Let the child stick the star on the chart for himself. This gives him a sense of worthiness and gets him actively participating in the class.

For older children and teens, object lessons are quite effective. Bring some props to class to illustrate verses. Keep your mind open, active, and innovative. Teens like to be challenged. (The concepts of sin and salvation are more effectively presented around the age of 8 or later for deaf children.)

The following material by Jeanne Manning may also be helpful in teaching deaf children:

The Teacher, Christ, is the greatest example we have and our lives should reflect His attributes if we are to be effective teachers in this complex world. All teachers should radiate these attributes but for those who work with deaf children these are a must.

1. Love—Without this characteristic there is no need for a person to consider teaching. Love is the supreme motive for teaching. A teacher can lack many other qualifications but love will be the greatest teaching aid he will ever have. A child knows if you truly love him or are teaching because of an obligation. Christ was motivated by love. The Scriptures often speak of His being moved with compassion as He observed various situations.

2. Be Enthusiastic—Get excited about your students and the material you are presenting. Express it as the greatest message in the world. Act excited; children love action. Put yourself into it. You may not feel it's part of your personality to be dramatic, but to convey truth to deaf children we often have to forget ourselves and try to communicate no matter how awkward we may feel at first. You may feel foolish but remember that the attention span of children is shorter than yours. To keep their attention you must keep it interesting by the way you express yourself with signs, facial expression, body movements, and your materials (lesson, visual aids, etc.).

3. Be in Control—Jesus was always in control of the situation and appeared poised and calm. Children know when you lose control, don't know how to handle a student, or are unprepared. Remember that God has placed you in your position and He will help you. Build your own confidence. God doesn't choose failures and He doesn't expect you to be one. A child should always be assured that "Teacher" is in control. Set limits for children. When they know their boundaries you will have a better class and much more learning will occur.

4. Be Approachable—Children (and adults) like to

feel their teacher is interested in them as individuals. Let them feel free to express their feelings toward you and situations in the classroom. If a child fears you or feels you don't love him he will seldom confide in you.

5. Be Optimistic—Believe in yourself and in your students, even the mentally slower ones. They will surprise you if you will expect more from them. Jesus believed in the disciples and taught them even though He often repeated himself. Jesus prepared these men for the day that He would leave them. When the time arrived they still couldn't understand where He was going and why they also couldn't go, but Christ was patient and optimistic with His pupils. He knew one day their understanding would be opened. Jesus did become frustrated with them, however, so don't be surprised if you do too!

6. Communicate With Your Father—Jesus talked to the Father about His pupils and so must we. Talk to Him about your own feelings of inferiority in teaching His Word and communicating His message. As we communicate we find answers.

Teaching for facts is easy, teaching for meaning isn't! Creative teachers focus on:

1. Meaning, not merely facts.

2. Making sure students are actively involved in exploring for meaning.

3. Stimulating and guiding students in the discovery process of learning.

Your curriculum materials are not your authority, God's Word is. Curriculum is not the answer; it is only a help.

The deaf child's language level is significantly lower than that of the hearing child of the same age.

You need to select curriculum for a younger language level but upgrade illustrations to fit the child's experience level. You may use a beginner quarterly with the intermediate child but don't insult him by letting him know this. Use the language level of the beginner but rewrite it to fit the age-level with whom you are working.

Understand the level of the children with whom you are working. This may require a bit of outside study. Study the developmental stages of the age-group. Know and understand this group psychologically but keep in mind that deaf children may be behind here. You need to know how they are developing physically at this stage and the kinds of activities they enjoy. These things will help you to develop better illustrations so the children will relate to the materials offered in the classroom.

Use your Christian bookstore. Use other peoples' ideas. No one says you have to be a genius; use other peoples' brains. Craft ideas are unlimited and there are many good books available on this subject. Christian comic books can even be good teaching aids. Mix and match visuals. Let your mind begin to develop its own ideas. Secular magazines can be a great source of pictures for crafts, visuals, visualized songs, and creative stories. Construction paper and glue are God's special gifts!

You can't have too many visuals! Almost anything can be used as a visual aid. Object lessons using household articles make great teaching aids. Gospel magic, puppets (use two-handed five-fingered ones so you can sign with them), pantomime, roleplaying, films, filmstrips, an overhead projector, maps, charts, flannelboards, newspapers, and chalkboards are just a few of the visuals you can utilize in the classroom for deaf children.

As in any type of ministry, you may wonder if you are really getting through to the children and young people. Take heart when you think your work is in vain; be patient. All God expects is your best and He will give the increase.

Now let us turn our attention to the backbone of the church—the adults. This group will include everyone from age 20 to 90 and every level of comprehension.Their signs may be somewhat old-fashioned, depending on their background. Sometimes if you use the newer instructional-type signs it may be offensive, so it is best to introduce them slowly or explain from the beginning that they may choose to ignore your instructional signs and just read the normal signs as if the other signs weren't there. If you are casual about this most people will not complain.

Most deaf adults are hungry for the Word of God and highly appreciative of those who teach them. They should have some part in deciding what is studied, even if you use nothing more than a "straw vote" to determine their interests. As discussed in chapter 9, it might be wise to offer more than one adult class and let them choose the level of teaching with which they feel most comfortable. It is usually unwise to use a quarterly that has a number indicating a grade level. No reference should be made to the comparable hearing level of education.

I have found the undated type of lessons works the best for adults because the teacher can be more innovative. Study questions may be compiled, passed out, and corrected by the class members themselves. I remember how proud our deaf were when they discovered they had answered all the questions correctly! A further advantage of using study questions is it helps the student get the textual content firmly in mind. If the material has to do with geographical locations, a blank map with places to write in the names of cities, mountains, valleys, or rivers also creates interest.

One of the most important aspects of any set of lessons is an understandable vocabulary. If you discover the students don't understand the material, you may need to prepare a list of words with their definitions. I realize this may be time-consuming for the teacher, but one who truly wants the deaf to learn is willing to do the extra work involved!

It is important that the Bible be used in the class by you and by the students. They need to understand that the references written in the quarterly are from the Bible and aren't just man's words. There are many translations and paraphrases available that are excellent for the deaf because of their readability. What is best for one group may not be best for your group.

One last word in closing this chapter: Religious education in the church means all the difference between strong Christians and weak ones! To be negligent in your duty to provide instruction in the Bible and the application of those principles to their lives is to be useless in the kingdom of God. "Like a mighty army, moves the church of God," but only if they are fed the Word of God, the Bread of Life.

12

Special Ministry Programs for the Deaf

In addition to providing regular weekly services for the deaf there are other areas that need to be emphasized. These areas are often overlooked and may be instrumental in reaching more deaf than the regular programs normally provided.

The first of these programs is a Vacation Bible School for the deaf during the summer months. The dates for this will have to be worked into the church calendar but it should not conflict with other programs for the deaf in the community. I know of few churches that provide this kind of program but it is an ideal situation because the deaf children are home from the residential schools and this may be the only time you have to reach them with the message of the gospel. It might be necessary to have it at the same time the hearing church has their Vacation Bible School but it would require separate classes, opening exercises, and so forth for the deaf children. If the deaf have their own it works better since you can take as much time as you need to demonstrate concepts.

A major problem is the lack of adequate personnel to operate such a program. It is much easier if you can find someone who does this as a summer ministry and who would come in with fresh ideas and materials and administer the whole program using the personnel you already have in the church.

It is wise to keep the lessons simple and nondenominational so as to be open to children of all churches. This will increase attendance and also promote the gospel.

It is important to have innovative directors and teachers who can pattern the lessons and materials to the comprehension level of the various groups of children and are proficient in the communication mode of the children, be it oral or using Total Communication. These aspects have already been discussed regarding religious education for the various groups in the previous chapter.

A second special program that is often overlooked is the youth program in a deaf church. Often the services and activities are geared only for the adults with the children and young people more or less expected to follow along. A golden opportunity lies ahead for the church that will provide a special program for the youth of the community, especially accelerated during the summer months when they are home from the residential schools and colleges. Many times they are unemployed during these months and are anxious for activities. They are often relegated to the television set and expected to be satisfied with that.

Naturally, the promotion of such a youth program needs the support of the parents. Assuming you have their addresses, visit the homes and tell the parents about it. If they will bring their children you might be able to provide transportation for the return trip home. Some churches provide transportation by way of a church bus route. The evening of the activities could be called Youth Night, Fellowship Night, etc. One necessity for the program is space for such sports as volleyball, dodge ball, horseshoe throwing, and so on. The deaf enjoy active sports, as do most young people.

Choose a night when the deaf of your community are relatively free for this program. This will vary from area to area. Allow approximately 2 hours for the activity-fun time.

Since this is a social time you could even provide a concession stand and sell or donate softdrinks and snacks. Maybe a concerned group in the church would want to provide these for the youth night. At the conclusion of the activity time present a brief skit or lesson with a spiritual theme. The young people will listen now that their physical energy is well spent. You will find that many will attend this type of a program who could not or would not attend church or Sunday school. This may be the only opportunity for them to hear the gospel.

As with all young people, you must first win their confidence. This may take a considerable amount of time but patience will pay off. When they discover you are truly interested in them and can communicate with them they will confide in you.

During the winter months, if you live in a cold climate, you can have indoor activities or snow activities outside with the latter part of the evening inside. Be sure to plan special activities during the time the young people are on vacation from school. If you use Bible games be sure to keep them basic and do not embarrass those who are limited in their Biblical knowledge. Many may not know the answers and refuse to even try lest they find themselves embarrassed by their ignorance.

It is a good idea to take the deaf young people with you to visit new prospects. They enjoy it and it breaks down the initial barriers. Remember to keep their parents informed since they are very concerned about where their children are.

As the young people become more and more interested in the group and the church and hear the others discussing the Sunday services they will desire to attend also.

Do not neglect any segment of the deaf church. Activity groups can be formed to parallel those of the hearing church regardless of age. The only necessity is that you have enough experienced personnel to deal with them. The church should be sensitive to meeting the needs of the deaf at every age-level.

DEAF CAMPS AND RETREATS

Deaf camps and/or retreats are very beneficial to the deaf and generally come under the jurisdiction of a district director. Occasionally several churches in close proximity may join together for a weekend retreat but primarily it works well to have the district director promote such activities. He has the time to do so, he has the contacts for the facilities, and (in conjunction with personnel operating the camps) he can usually provide better coordination of facilities. If you are not a district-appointed director and wish to promote, plan, and lead such a camp the following information may be of help.

The place to begin is at the district level. With the approval of the district officers dates can be set to coordinate with the other district camps. It should be noted that rarely can these plans be made on the spur of the moment but, rather, need to be placed on the calendar a full year or more in advance. After securing the date and campground facilities a price must be set for the campers. This varies from district to district depending on the type of facilities, meals provided, personnel required to operate it (caretaker, nurse, night watchmen), insurance, and so on.

Staffing is generally quite simple since you merely use the workers within the confines of your district. You can use trainees as teachers' aides and cabin counselors. It is always nice to provide outside (out-of-state) teachers and ministers for the sake of variety. If finances do not permit this, you could use available area ministers at much less expense.

When planning a camp, one person may be the key to whether the campers return next year—that person is the cook. Tasty, well-planned, and well-prepared meals are a must. Campers can be tolerant of many inconveniences but when it comes to the meals they have a long memory. An ample supply of provisions must also be assured. No camper should leave the dining hall hungry or have to drive to a nearby community to supplement what he receives at the camp.

It is wise also to have a business manager who takes care of collecting all the funds and disbursing them to those who should receive them. All should be paid by check or the business manager should receive a receipt when the bill is paid. Insurance is a must for all camp activities. Make sure you know who is covered, for how long, and where. Some insurance policies do not cover the camper when he's outside the campground.

Advertising and promotion for the camp should follow the guidelines for any normal church activity. Just remember to keep the cost of the camp as low as possible and ask for donations from parishioners to pay for the few who may not be able to afford to attend. It is helpful to provide transportation to and from the camp.

Remember, you will have both oral deaf and those who use Total Communication. You will need to separate these two groups for educational reasons. I have had to minister with both groups combined and I was never sure they all received what they should have out of it. It is profitable if the Scripture verses and the sermon or lesson outline are presented visually. Use butcher paper and a felt-tip pen and print large so it can be read from a reasonable distance.

The size of your group and the variety of the campers will determine the number of classes you will have. Be sure to plan for more classes than necessary and keep them rather small. If less campers show up it is easier to combine or cancel a class than to find a teacher and start a new class after camp begins.

Organization is the key to a successful camp. How smoothly it operates will dictate the tone of the camp and the campers will feel secure if they see the director, counselors, and teachers know their individual responsibilities and perform them well. Suggested classes and ages are as follows: adults (25 and up); young adults (17-25); teenagers (13-16); junior high (11-12); junior (10-11); beginners (9-10); and children up to age 9. You need not limit class members to exact ages if you feel they should be in a different class due to language levels. It is wise not to attempt to include the very young deaf in the classes since their language is not developed enough so they could profit much from it. It would also be a good idea to offer a sign language class for hearing adults.

Materials for classes can be devised from Vacation Bible School material or other appropriate visuals. Remember to choose teachers who can prepare their own lessons. Innovativeness is the key since instruction must be individualized for the deaf.

Retreats are normally operated on a short-term basis (for example, Friday evening, all day Saturday, and Sunday until after the noon meal). They can be held any time of the year but it is wise to choose a time when there aren't too many other activities on the church calendar. Many churches have facilities for winter retreats and the winter is a wonderful time to have one. Again, the district calendar and officials must be consulted and the planning for the retreat will pattern somewhat that of a camp. One special speaker is usually sufficient with a short course of instruction for the Saturday and Sunday class sessions. If finances are limited the speaker could even be a pastor to the deaf from the immediate area.

In conclusion, let me emphasize that whether it be in a camp program, retreat, or the regular activities of the church, in an atmosphere of warm Christian fellowship the deaf are teachable and inspiring to be around. When you give your church people an opportunity to reach out to those around them you will find they do not have time to become disgruntled and unhappy and cause discord in your church.

13

Developing Administrative Models for the Deaf Ministry

Open communication, sensitivity, teachableness (regardless of rank or office), and having a finger on the pulse of deaf ministry in the nation are the key to successful administration of any program for the deaf, regardless of denomination.

Church organizations have a "chain of command" with which to be reckoned. If the channels of communication are open from the bottom to the top, and there is a real burden for what is best for the deaf, then we will be successful. It has always been my opinion that there is wisdom in numbers. In other words, a committee of several knowledgeable leaders is better than a dictator who may make expensive mistakes for the health of the kingdom of God. However, it is clear from Scripture that when God wanted to accomplish specific tasks He sent a man—Jesus, John the Baptist, the disciples, Paul. But we must recognize these were not ordinary people; they were led by the Holy Spirit!

Let us consider each of the levels of administration, then discuss how each one works with the others. Since this book is aimed at any minister of the deaf regardless of denomination, you will have to change the titles of these persons or groups to fit your specific organization. This discussion is not intended to advocate one organization over another, but rather to look at administrative models that will enhance ministry to the deaf.

It matters not whether the head at a national headquarters is named superintendent, overseer, or bishop. Such a person cannot possibly become personally involved with every aspect of the ministries of the church he serves. For this reason a national representative is needed to oversee the unique ministry to the deaf.

I say "unique" because I know of no other group that needs such specialized attention as the deaf. Since they are a subculture, they have different comprehension levels, psychological concerns, and sociological concerns and the ministry to the deaf must consider all of these. This is no small task. Whoever becomes this national representative must try to keep all of these concerns in focus.

You will note that I did not say the person needs to be proficient in all of these areas. Good administration depends on his gathering around him knowledgeable people who can make up for his own insufficiencies (in no way meant to be derogatory). In other words, a person who is really concerned about the deaf needs only to consult those who know their needs and relevant concerns. It is amazing to watch God work through this method.

This national representative should be mobile enough so he/she can visit the various areas of the nation and keep the pulse of the deaf groups, yet be accessible enough so ministers or prospective ministers to the deaf can visit for counsel and guidance. Such a person can also in a general way encourage the production of literature, quarterlies, religious tracts, or informational brochures for educating both the churches and the general public about the deaf.

It has always been my opinion that two people could better accomplish this task, one in the office and one on the field. At any rate, it is not a simple task and takes a consecrated and dedicated person who will spend a great deal of time orienting his colleagues both above and below him about the needs of the deaf and the uniqueness of this ministry.

In most organizations the national office is not in a position to dictate the terms of the deaf ministry so let us look at the next level, the district. (Some call it a diocese, conference, or synod.) This level consists of several officers who are elected or chosen by their colleagues for the administration of the denomination within certain geographical borders (an area of one state, several states, or part of a state).

The same situation prevails at this level as at the national level. One who desires to minister to the deaf is met with the task of sharing his burden of ministry with these men and women, orienting them to the uniqueness of it, and hopefully convincing them of the necessity of appointing a district director. Assuming this is accomplished, this district director would oversee the various deaf groups in the district and assist in counseling and advising the interpreters, lay preachers, or ordained ministers laboring in these deaf churches.

The director could also, on a "circuit-rider" basis, establish classes in sign language or short-term training programs in churches interested in beginning a ministry to the deaf. Afterwards he could be instrumental in procuring personnel for the continuation of the work. This may sound easy but it isn't since there is a great dearth of religious workers in all denominations and in the secular realm as well. Teachers, social workers, vocational rehabilitation counselors, etc. are all in short supply when it comes to working with the deaf.

Now we come to the next level, the local church. This level may be headed by a variety of personnel depending on the size of the deaf group and the availability of personnel. The leader may be an interpreter, lay preacher, Sunday school teacher who also interprets services, or a deaf lay person who takes charge of the group but depends on a hearing interpreter to interpret services. We have already discussed the relationship between these individuals and the pastor of the church with which they may be affiliated.

Now let us look at the relationship of these administrators with each other. If there is open communication at all levels a great deal of the problems are resolved. Misunderstandings come from a lack of clear communication without hidden nuances of meanings that need further interpretation or clarification. Such bureaucratic red tape bogs down the work of God and alienates people from each other.

This is closely linked with my next word, *sensitivity*. Unfortunately, in some areas of society this word has negative connotations due to the encounter or T-groups of a few years ago, but on the Christian plane it is very important. Not only should the Christian be sensitive to the leading of the Holy Spirit and the will of God in his life, but he also should be sensitive to the feelings of those to whom he ministers and *with whom* he ministers. Far too many have fallen away from ministry to the deaf because of insensitive people who discounted their efforts rather than counseling and advising them in a constructive way. Hurt feelings have caused many to give up any attempt to minister to these who need it so desparately.

To be amenable is to be cooperative and humble. If a person is amenable he will accept with humility and gracefulness suggestions, criticisms, and counsel from those in authority over him. At the same time the administrator must remember that it is not always *what* he says but *how* he says it that makes the difference.

There seems to be an unwritten code that says authority means "I tell the other person what to do and he does it without questioning." That may work well in the military but not in the ministry. Asking always accomplishes more than ordering! Ministry to the deaf is so delicate that each needs to work in harmony with the other whether the person is above or below him in the hierarchy of organization.

Through the years of my deaf ministry I have had the opportunity to observe many deaf groups, camps, and secular organizations. I have noticed that when jealousies begin to surface the effectiveness of the organization declines. As administrator, pastor, lay worker, or interpreter we must be careful not to alienate ourselves from other deaf groups. I know of some who refuse to fellowship with another church lest they "steal" the sheep. Or they refuse to participate in a joint effort in a district camp because of one reason or another. Such jealousies can be resolved by open communication and sensitivity.

"Let each esteem other better than themselves . . ." (Philippians 2:3). Never belittle the other minister to the deaf. He may be doing a greater job for God than you. Only God can be the judge.

In conclusion, regardless of the administrative level at which you find yourself, keep those in authority above and below you *informed!* Let them know what you are doing, what you have done, and what you are planning to do. In this way all can work together without overlapping efforts and in harmony with each other.

Epilogue

After reading this book I trust you have been stirred to open the doors of your church to a ministry to the deaf. If you cannot do it within your own church, I encourage you to at least support those who are actively engaged in it.

I rest my case. . . . The opportunity and an "open door" awaits those who will accept the challenge.

Edgar D. Lawrence

Notes

[1]Jerome Schein and Marcus Delk, *The Deaf Population of the United States* (Silver Spring, MD: National Association of the Deaf, 1974), p. 4.

[2]A. G. Ward, *The Minister and His Work* (Springfield, MO: Gospel Publishing House, 1945), p. 12.

[3]See *Sign Language Made Simple* by E. D. Lawrence (Springfield, MO: Gospel Publishing House, 1976).

[4]H. D. Babbidge, *Education of the Deaf* (a report to the Secretary of Health, Education, and Welfare by an advisory committee on the education of the deaf; U.S. Department of Health, Education, and Welfare, Washington, D.C., 1964).

[5]See Undated Deaf Manuals published by the Gospel Publishing House, 1445 Boonville, Springfield, MO 65802.

[6]McCay Vernon and Eugene D. Mindel, *They Grow in Silence* (Silver Spring, MD: National Association of the Deaf, 1971), p. x.

[7]Dr. McCay Vernon is a psychologist, Dr. Eugene D. Mindel and Dr. Hilde Schlesinger are child psychiatrists, and Dr. Kaye Meadows is a sociologist.

[8]Dr. David M. Denton, Superintendent of the Maryland School for the Deaf.

[9]Shein and Delk, *op. cit.*

[10]*Ibid.*, p. 83.

[11]Babbidge, *op. cit.*

[12]Illinois, Indiana, Iowa, Kansas, Michigan, Minnesota, Missouri, Nebraska, North Dakota, Ohio, South Dakota, and Wisconsin.

[13]Connecticut, Maine, Massachusetts, New Hampshire, New Jersey, New York, Pennsylvania, Rhode Island, and Vermont.